THE DAY AFTER he was inaugurated, President Donald Trump visited the CIA and announced that his attacks on the media would continue. "I have a running war with the media. They are among the most dishonest human beings on earth, right?" he said.

The next week, his advisor, Steve Bannon, told the *New York Times* that the media had been "humiliated" by the paper's biased 2016 election coverage. "I want you to quote this," he said. "The media here is the opposition party. They don't understand this country. They still do not understand why Donald Trump is the president of the United States."

On February 17, Trump tweeted to his twenty-five million followers that the "fake news media" is "not my enemy, it is the enemy of the American People!" He reiterated this in a public speech a week later, making sure to clarify he was singling out "fake news."

NBC News political director Chuck Todd responded on social media: "This not a laughing matter. I'm sorry, delegitimizing the press

is unAmerican." Journalists wrote tributes to themselves about the importance of journalism, and shared the most indignant reactions to Trump on social media. Many media outlets and editors said the president's insults were renewing their sense of mission. The *Washington Post* changed its motto to "Democracy dies in darkness." The *New York Times* ran an ad campaign claiming, "The truth is more important than ever," a statement indicating that for the paper the importance of truth was conditional on whether its management agreed with the politician in charge.

The media shouldn't have been surprised by what Trump was doing. In speeches and on social media throughout the campaign, Trump played the part of a busy media critic, calling various news outlets fake, disgusting, and dishonest. His frequent attacks on the media were lapped up by voters, frustrated by years of uneven coverage of conservative politicians and issues. Media outlets spent much of 2016 absolutely trashing Trump and assuring viewers and readers that Hillary

Donald Trump's frequent attacks on the media were lapped up by voters, frustrated by years of uneven coverage of conservative politicians and issues.

Clinton would easily be elected. Trump pulled off a surprise victory that demonstrated the chasm between half of the electorate and the national political media.

The media should have made short-term systematic changes to its news-gathering process to make sure that it would never again be so out of touch with the Americans it covers. Instead, it reacted even more hysterically, pushing conspiracy theories that Trump had won because of a scourge of fake news or Russian meddling. Believing its anti-Trump coverage had been too limited during the campaign, the media began on all-out assault of negative news against him, pushing dozens of what turned out to be false stories, such as those suggesting that transgender teen suicide rates had spiked in the immediate aftermath of Trump's election, that three states had had their elections hacked, that Trump's treasury secretary nominee had foreclosed on a ninety-year-old woman for a twenty-seven-cent payment error, that federal agencies were purging scientific data from websites, that Trump had removed a bust of Martin Luther King Jr. from the White House, and that top management at the State Department had resigned in protest.

The response to Trump's election from the media has been an admixture of anger and confusion. For decades, the press in America has been accorded a variety of perks and privileges based on the assumptions that it was integral to the success of civil society and that it would exercise its power responsibly. However, Trump's victory has advanced the developing realization among many Americans that the media has completely abdicated its responsibility and shown itself hostile to the values and ideas many Americans hold. Much of the population no longer believes the media should be treated deferentially and given the power to shape, much less control, public opinion.

How'd We Get Here?

Complaining vociferously about the press is a Republican tradition dating back at least to Dwight Eisenhower's 1964 convention speech. Ike received a prolonged standing ovation when he said, "Let us particularly scorn the divisive efforts of those outside our family, including sensation-seeking columnists and commentators, because I assure you that these are people who couldn't care less about the good of our party."

At nearly every appearance President George H. W. Bush made during his unsuccessful reelection campaign in 1992, he would display his favorite bumper sticker: "Annoy the media: Re-elect Bush." The crowd would hoot and holler as Bush complained about a media that clearly signaled its preference for Bill Clinton.

Political candidates as different as Richard Nixon and John McCain made similar complaints. Conservative radio talk-show hosts spent decades dissecting the framing and spin of stories in the major media. Conservatives complained so much about media bias that it almost became trite. Liberal media critics such as Eric Alterman – who authored the 2003 book *What Liberal Media?*, which attempted to rebut GOP charges of media bias – said complaints about the media were little more than conservatives "playing the referees." Whatever the case, journalists accepted the complaints as a part of doing business and made little to no apparent effort to improve.

In fact, they got worse.

At some point, something broke. The regular complaints about media bias were harder to ignore as the problems became more obvious. The episodes of major media malpractice are simply too numerous to list, but a few stand out for having a profound impact on undermining Americans' institutional trust in the news media.

In 2005, Hurricane Katrina hit the Gulf and led to what Dan Rather – yes, the former *CBS News* anchor who pushed fraudulent documents to discredit George W. Bush – called "one of the quintessential great moments in television news." Yet, media critic W. Joseph Campbell wrote in *Getting It Wrong: Debunking the Greatest Myths in American Journalism* that the erroneous and over-the-top reporting on Katrina "had the cumulative the effect of painting for America and the rest of the world a scene of surreal violence and terror, something straight out of *Mad Max* or *Lord of the Flies*." This reporting pushed racist stereotypes, scaremongering, and a political focus that emphasized national control over local solutions.

Typical of the media's antipathy to Republicans, the national news coverage laid seemingly all the problems with the hurricane response at the foot of President George W. Bush. While the Bush administration was not above criticism, comparatively little blame for the dysfunctional disaster response was placed on Louisiana's notoriously corrupt and incompetent state and local governments, which at the time were predominantly Democratic. The mayor of New Orleans during Hurricane Katrina would go to prison in 2014 for taking hundreds of thousands of dollars in bribes from city contractors, and this corruption began well before Katrina. At the time of his sentencing, Nagin was the seventeenth elected official from the New Orleans area to be convicted on federal corruption or fraud charges since the hurricane.

In 2006, an exotic dancer hired by members of the Duke University lacrosse team alleged she'd been violently gang-raped. A year later, the three men she'd accused were not just found not guilty but actually declared innocent as the case completely fell apart. In the interim, many major media outlets reported on the story in a biased and hysterical fashion, convicting the three men of rape, racism, and a host of other sins in the court of public opinion. The media used the episode to force a national conversation about the need to accept all manner of politically correct liberal pieties.

New York Times public editor Dan Okrent criticized his paper's Duke coverage in 2007. Speaking about it years later, he stated: "It was white over black, it was male over female, it was rich over poor, educated over uneducated. All the things that we know happen in the world coming together in one place and journalists, they start to quiver with a thrill when something like this happens." Okrent's comments weren't terribly representative of widespread media concern, however. Since

---

Complaining vociferously about the press is a Republican tradition dating back at least to Dwight Eisenhower's 1964 convention speech.

---

the Duke case fell apart, there's been comparatively little reflection about the dangers of self-righteous Democratic prosecutors run amok or the need for the media to focus on facts and evidence when it is tempted to indulge narratives that comport with its biased perceptions.

In 2009, a Tea Party movement began to push back against what its participants perceived as radical policies in the Obama administration pointed toward the growth and centralization of the federal government. The backlash was almost entirely predictable. Obama campaigned as a centrist and pragmatist, but once elected he governed like a socialist ideologue. His first two major legislative moves involved creating a trillion-dollar spending bill that was supposed to rescue the economy from the depths of recession but disproportionately rewarded Democratic special interests. Not only was the economy not rescued, it never recovered – after eight years Obama was the first president in modern American history who never had a year of

GDP growth over 3 percent. Obama's second major legislative move was the sprawling two-thousand-page bill to nationalize health care known as Obamacare, which has been a rolling disaster ever since it was implemented and has triggered a number of alarming regulatory restrictions and court decisions enhancing federal power. Additionally, Obama brazenly lied about the fact that the proposed law would kick millions of Americans off their existing health insurance plans.

In retrospect, Tea Party concerns about Obama's nascent presidency were entirely grounded in legitimate objections that his expensive schemes would fail and do great harm to the notion of limited government. Nonetheless, the media treated these legitimate concerns as the contemptuous and irrational yawps of the racist Republican grassroots.

The Tea Party movement was launched by the impassioned plea of CNBC journalist Rick Santelli, yet fell into major mainstream media opposition. An early CNN report featured reporter Susan Roesgen fighting with participants about their views on the president's policies. She described the event as "anti-government, anti-CNN since this is highly promoted by the right-wing conservative network Fox." Roesgen was let go by CNN, but negative and dismissive coverage continued as the protest movement grew. In one case, completely unsubstantiated claims of racial slurs and spitting on Congressmen were given wide play by the media. Protesters who showed up at town halls were disparaged as mentally unhinged and possibly violent.

And though voter concerns about the media were treated as pure paranoia, there was mounting evidence that the media was engaged in conspiratorial behavior designed to target those resistant to advancing a liberal policy agenda. In 2010, a secret e-mail list called "Journolist" was revealed. During the 2008 campaign, hundreds of journalists used it to shape narratives to help then–Democratic candidate Barack Obama. Participants, who included mainstream reporters as well as overtly liberal journalists, discussed how to suppress negative information about Obama's longtime pastor Jeremiah Wright. Ideas included attacking conservatives as racist. One contributor said, "If the right forces us all to either defend Wright or tear him down, no matter what we choose, we lose the game they've put upon us. Instead, take one of them – Fred Barnes, Karl Rove who cares – and call them racists." Another discussion compared members of the Tea Party movement to Nazis.

The relationship between the media and conservatives continued to sour after that. On July 31, 2012, Republican candidate for president Mitt Romney paid his respects at Poland's Tomb of the Unknown Soldier in Warsaw. He was making an international trip as part of his presidential campaign. Campaign reporters had all agreed, for some reason, that Romney had made horrific campaign-ending mistakes by saying security problems at the London Olympics were "disconcerting," referring formally instead of casually to Labour leader Ed Miliband, and revealing he had taken a meeting with the secretive MI-6 agency. At the time, Romney shook hands with military veterans and chatted with Warsaw's mayor. As he made his way to his vehicle, a group of reporters from top media outlets began screaming.

"Governor Romney are you concerned about some of the mishaps of your trip?" a CNN reporter shouted. A *Washington Post* reporter famously shrieked, "What about your gaffes?" And a *New York Times* reporter yelled the follow-up question: "Governor Romney, do you feel that your gaffes have overshadowed your foreign trip?"

A few months later, when Romney was critical of the Obama administration's handling of the Benghazi attack that killed four Americans, including an ambassador, the media immediately pushed back, suggesting that the real problem was Romney's critique. The Obama administration falsely placed blame for the attack on anger at an American filmmaker's work critical of Islam, and the media by and large accepted these outlandish claims. Obama officials put out videos in other countries claiming that Americans were not to disparage other religions, despite the First Amendment protecting the right of Americans to do just that. Moderating a presidential debate, political reporter Candy Crowley helped President Obama when Mitt Romney had him on the ropes regarding his handling of the aftermath of the terror attack, taking Obama's side in suggesting that the presidential administration always clearly regarded it as a coordinated terrorist attack instead of a riot in response to a video. The Obama administration's position on what caused Benghazi would have been clarified by a *60 Minutes* interview the day after the incident that had Obama refusing to rule out the possibility Benghazi was a terrorist attack, but *60 Minutes*, likely well aware it would hurt his reelection chances, didn't broadcast the interview – and instead quietly released a transcript of Obama's remarks a few days before the election. In trying to explain the extraordinary deference on Benghazi of *CBS News*, it helps to know that Obama's deputy national security adviser, Ben Rhodes – the same man who would later brag in the pages of the *New York Times* about dishonestly manipulating reporters to pass the Iran nuclear deal – is the brother of *CBS News* president David Rhodes.

In another debate, Mitt Romney talked about his efforts to bring more women into

---

Even someone as previously beloved by the media as John McCain was slowly transformed by biased characterizations into a Hitler-like representation.

---

public service while he was governor. He said that he combed through binders full of resumes of qualified women to accomplish his goal of increasing the number of women in the workforce.

Somehow this became another media obsession, where "binders full of women" became shorthand for Mitt Romney's alleged misogyny. On October 12, 2016, in the midst of an uproar over Donald Trump's sexually offensive commentary caught on an old tape, Matt Viser, the deputy Washington bureau chief for the *Boston Globe*, would write that "'Binders full of women' – a comment about resumes of female applicants for state government jobs – seems, at this point, quite quaint." Yet, like so many of his peers, Viser spent much of the 2012 campaign pushing the Obama campaign's messaging that "binders full of women" meant Mitt Romney had problems with women.

Naturally, the accusations of misogyny were nothing compared to the charges of racism. Romney ran ads correctly pointing out that the Obama administration had issued rules gutting the wildly popular welfare reform legislation that was broadly agreed to have dramatically reduced the size of America's welfare rolls. It didn't matter that Robert Rector, the policy wonk who wrote the welfare reform legislation, said Romney was correct. Instead, media "fact-checkers" badly mangled the details of the legislation and the media seized on the misinformation to make ridiculous claims that Romney was making coded appeals to racism. This devolved to the point of a television shouting match between MSNBC's Chris Matthews and then–Republican National Committee head Reince Priebus, where Matthews accused Priebus of playing the "race card" for saying that "work requirements" should be a part of receiving welfare benefits.

What happened to Mitt Romney was sadly typical of what has happened to all Republican candidates for high office. Even someone as previously beloved by the media as John McCain was slowly transformed by biased characterizations into a Hitler-like representation during his campaign against Barack Obama in 2008. But when it happened to Mitt Romney – a squeaky clean, unfailingly nice, completely moderate Mormon from Massachusetts – Republicans realized that the media would do it to anyone.

The problems continued in the second Obama term, as additional scandals came out but were barely covered, much less given the regular breathless attention political scandals are normally given. When Internal Revenue Service officials revealed that actors in the agency, some of whom were in frequent contact with the White House, had targeted conservative opponents of Obama and limited their ability to gain tax-exempt status, it was treated as if it were not a huge deal. This largely passed under the radar, even though for many Americans it was a scandal that eclipsed Watergate many times over.

Not Just Politics

The media problems weren't just about politics, either. Media bias reached a critical mass where it was seen as a fundamental threat to the cherished traditions, values, and religion of millions of Americans. Media figures couldn't hide their contempt for Americans who did not share the same progressive values as them. Shortly after he retired as editor of the *New York Times* in 2011, Bill Keller gave a speech in Austin, Texas, about the paper's bias. He said it was crucial for coverage of politics to be balanced and fair at the paper, but revealed that when it came to moral and social issues, that was a different matter altogether.

Asked directly if the *Times* slanted its coverage to favor "Democrats and liberals," he added: "Aside from the liberal values, sort of social values thing that I talked about, no, I don't think that it does." He was admitting the paper didn't care about biased coverage when it came to little things like whether marriage, the bedrock institution of society, should be redefined or whether ending human life in the womb should be allowed throughout all nine months of pregnancy.

At the time, the paper was in the midst of a decades-long major media campaign to redefine marriage to include same-sex couples. It was also in the middle of decades of struggles to cover religion well, particularly traditional religion. That struggle was still going on in December 2016 when executive editor Dean Baquet admitted, "We don't get religion." (He got that right; a *New York Times* report from eight months before the time of this writing claiming that the New Testament "calls for the execution of gays" remains on the paper's website uncorrected, despite being called out for being wildly wrong by numerous prominent outlets and religious voices.) And the paper has never been known for covering the abortion topic well, either.

When David Shaw wrote his landmark exposé in the *Los Angeles Times* in 1990 about the level of bias of major media in favor of abortion, "Abortion Bias Seeps into News," the *New York Times* was one of the publications whose slant on abortion was already legendary.

Shaw's well-researched look at the topic mentions that the media uses language that frames the abortion debate in terms favorable to those who support the practice, quotes abortion-rights advocates more frequently and favorably than opponents, and ignores or gives minimal attention to events and issues favorable to abortion opponents.

That's exactly what happened in 2013 when Philadelphia abortionist Kermit Gosnell was on trial for the murders of a woman and some of the children whose lives he ended in his filthy clinic. He kept trophies of baby feet in jars. His employees testified that he snipped the spinal cords of children he'd just delivered. He performed abortions without sufficient painkillers for poor immigrant women. His clinic was soaked in cat urine and so messy that medical teams couldn't evacuate patients safely. He kept fetal parts in the refrigerator next to employee lunches.

It had all the makings of a major media maelstrom: a prolific serial murderer, a sensational trial, innocent victims. It even had angles for noncrime reporters, with troubling issues surrounding drugs, clinic regulations, immigration status, and racism.

Yet the media had to be shamed into giving the story more than a cursory mention. And even when major outlets devoted a bit of coverage to it here and there, the coverage was reluctant and paltry. One *Washington Post* reporter who had written dozens upon dozens of stories favorable to abortion-rights groups said that she hadn't covered the Gosnell incident because it was a "local crime story." The idea that national media doesn't cover local crime would be news to people who have read about the Newtown, Connecticut, shootings; the Trayvon Martin killing; the police shooting of Michael Brown in Ferguson, Missouri; or the riots in Baltimore.

On other social issues the bias was also clear. When the Supreme Court redefined marriage to include same-sex couples in a tight ruling condemned by the dissenters as a dangerous threat to rule of law and religious liberty, many media outlets responded by cheering the ruling, downplaying its threats, and even changing their logos to include pro–gay marriage imagery. *Washington Post* ombudsman Patrick Pexton wrote a 2013 column in response to a reader's plea that the paper publish journalism instead of advocacy and propaganda on the issue. In the article, Pexton characterized those who uphold marriage as the institution built around sexual complementarity as the equivalent of racists, admitted he didn't even know or understand the arguments in favor of defining marriage as the union of man and woman, and defended the paper's one-sided coverage as a matter of justice.

Whether the topic has been religion, the family, human life, guns, conservative governance, or even sports, the media bias has become more pronounced and the trouble with accuracy, an epidemic. Once conservatives saw the problems, they couldn't unsee them, even in the case of more nuanced issues, such as the media downplaying massive annual prolife marches while hyping Leftist marches, reacting hysterically to disasters that occur during Republican presidencies while giving the benefit of the doubt to the handling of oil spills or natural disasters that occur during Democratic tenures, spinning comments made by Republicans as sexist and bigoted while downplaying or trying to provide exculpatory context for charged comments by Democrats, using anonymous sources to tear down political opponents,

---

When the Supreme Court redefined marriage, many media outlets responded by cheering the ruling, downplaying its threats, and even changing their logos to include pro–gay marriage imagery.

---

hiding balancing viewpoints at the end of stories instead of featuring them more prominently in the text, using terms with negative connotations for causes that it dislikes and terms with positive connotations for those it favors, and finding other ways of shading the truth.

Looked at from the perspective of conservative voters who feel that they have been repeatedly lied to and abused by media elites for decades, it's not hard to understand how we ended up with President Trump. The media, however, is so unrepentant and lacking in self-awareness that it is having real trouble admitting it's done anything wrong, and instead is indulging its worst impulses of hyperbole and hysteria. The fact remains that the current political situation is the logical result of the hostile and distrustful environment it cultivated, rather than some black-swan event unleashed by the sudden onset of irrationality of voters in flyover states.

It was the media's decades-long approach of putting its thumb on the scale by covering conservatives and conservative causes poorly that created a lose-lose situation for conservatives. There was no way for them to operate successfully in a system where the media allowed them to be respected as the principled opposition only as long as they were shackled and limited by biased news coverage. And conservative voters were beyond sick of it. The media would say things that weren't true and cover issues dishonestly, and then accuse others of being liars or gaffe-makers for disagreeing. No candidate – not even squeaky-clean moderates like Mitt Romney – would keep the media from painting Republicans and their beliefs as dangerous. It was enough to make half the country give up on the enterprise of working with the media altogether.

Most Americans had no way to combat media crimes and their power to shape the culture and electoral outcomes, particularly if they were focused on their work and home life. And even most politicians weren't quite capable of combating this media power.

Along came Trump, the brilliant master of exploiting public opinion. A New York real estate developer and reality TV celebrity, he had spent decades studying the media and how to make it work to his advantage. Understanding that conservatives had lost trust in the credibility of the media to cover politics accurately, the media became one of his primary targets, and he played it like a fiddle. Trump voters loved that he was beating up the bully they had been impotent to vanquish. They loved that he destroyed the media's power to declare things gaffes, much less campaign-destroying gaffes. Figures such as Chuck Todd can lament Trump's ability to put the media in its place as being "un-American" all he wants. The fact is that Trump wouldn't have this power had the media not set things up through decades of shoddy coverage targeting its political opponents. The media did this to itself.

Trump's unique power to bring attention to the problems of the media also meant that his 2016 campaign proved a case study in identifying and examining pernicious media trends. Among the trends he identified that are worth exploring are the media's overwhelming desire to push narratives in spite of its inability to see the future; its undeniable coordination with the Democratic party; its attempts to present opinions as facts, and vice versa; and the blatant double standards in its coverage motivated by partisanship.

OBJECTIVITY AND OVERCONFIDENCE

While a few reporters here and there resisted the tide, there's no point in pretending that the media covered Donald Trump in a fair or nonhistrionic fashion. *New York Times* media writer Jim Rutenberg said what most journalists were thinking in his front-page August 8, 2016, article "Trump Is Testing the Norms of Objectivity in Journalism."

"If you're a working journalist and you believe that Donald J. Trump is a demagogue playing to the nation's worst racist and nationalistic tendencies, that he cozies up to anti-American dictators and that he would be dangerous with control of the United States nuclear codes, how the heck are you supposed to cover him?" Rutenberg asked. The premise was that most journalists would inevitably agree that Trump was a dangerous demagogue, and that they should continue to stay on the Trump beat even though they were unable or unwilling to change their opinion. If a reporter viewed Trump's presidency as "potentially dangerous," his reporting should reflect that, Rutenberg said.

He advised reporters to "throw out the textbook American journalism has been using," move away from a model of balanced coverage, and become openly oppositional. He acknowledged that such a change would "throw the advantage" to Hillary Clinton and he acknowledged that supporters of Trump would take an even-worse view of the media. Journalism shouldn't try so hard to be fair but instead "stand up to history's judgment" and "ferret out what the candidates will be like in the most powerful office in the world," he said.

What does that even mean? How could reporters speculate on the future? And why would they try? In his 2002 "Why Speculate?" speech, novelist Michael Crichton stated, "Because we are confronted by speculation at every turn, in print, on video, on the net, in conversation, we may eventually conclude that it must have value. But it doesn't. Because no matter how many people are speculating, no matter how familiar their faces, how good their makeup and how well they are lit, no matter how many weeks they appear before us in person or in columns, it remains true that none of them knows what the future holds."

New York Times executive editor Dean Baquet didn't condemn the approach Rutenberg advocated but praised it. "I thought Jim Rutenberg's column nailed it," he said in an interview with Harvard's NiemanLab.

The general media consensus was to speculate that Trump would be a bad president. Therefore, it justified increasingly negative coverage of Trump, and kinder coverage of Clinton. To talk honestly about both candidates' negative traits was derided by journalists as "false equivalence," since one candidate was, in its mind, worse than the other.

But not only was Crichton right about

speculation being largely worthless, the self-righteousness and misplaced confidence that accompanies so much media speculation is definitively discrediting. Never has this been more obvious than in the 2016 presidential campaign. The media felt empowered to take sides, because, to paraphrase the last president, it thought it had the power to determine who is on the right side of history. Voters had other ideas.

It was decided early on in newsrooms that Hillary Clinton would easily trounce Donald Trump. From the moment Trump announced his candidacy in June 2015, it was treated as a

---

The media felt empowered to take sides because it thought it had the power to determine who was on the right side of history. Voters had other ideas.

---

joke. Even after he won the Republican primary, besting many strong competitors, the general narrative was that he would not beat Clinton. The *New York Times* gave Clinton an 85 percent shot of winning. Statistician Nate Silver was lambasted by other liberals for giving Clinton only a 71.4 percent chance of winning. In turn, several prominent left-leaning media outlets went so far as to criticize Silver for not rating Clinton's chances of winning the election high enough. Surely, the prediction of the *Huffington Post* polls that Clinton had a 98 percent chance of winning has earned a prominent place in the annals of worthless speculation. The *New York Times* had a probability gauge that fluctuated throughout election night as results came in. It was in the 9:00 P.M. hour in the East that it began to look like Trump had a real chance of winning. The liberal hosts and talking heads on the news couldn't conceal their sadness and anger that night as the reality sunk in.

And yet, they had dropped their journalistic standards as they tried to elect Clinton, justifying the departure from even a pretense of objectivity on the grounds that Trump was dangerous, and they had lost. Their team had lost. And it was increasingly clear that Democrats were their team.

Team Democrat

The 2016 campaign featured the unauthorized release of e-mails from Democratic officials and Hillary Clinton campaign operatives via WikiLeaks, a group that publishes private or classified information from anonymous sources. The leak revealed details about how these officials interacted with the media, including journalists at CNN, POLITICO, the *Wall Street Journal*, and the *Washington Post*. This included information about a Democratic operative and former CNN contributor, Donna Brazile, repeatedly leaking debate questions that would be featured in a debate hosted by CNN to Hillary Clinton; a POLITICO reporter running the text of stories by Clinton operatives before publishing them; and a *New York Times* reporter allowing the Clinton campaign to nix an unflattering quote from an interview, contravening the newspaper's official policy forbidding quote approval.

The information once again confirmed the view of many Republicans that the media was at times behaving as the communications arm of the Democratic Party.

There can be little doubt that the media worked hand in glove with the Clinton campaign. A good example of how close the relationship worked took place with the media coverage of efforts to highlight Clinton's support from beauty pageant winner Alicia Machado.

At the end of the first presidential debate of 2016, Hillary Clinton shoehorned in a reference to the former beauty contestant who had won a contest run by Trump in 1997.

Trying to show Trump's misogyny, which was another major campaign theme of hers, she said, "And one of the worst things he said was about a woman in a beauty contest. He loves beauty contests, supporting them and hanging around them. And he called this woman 'Miss Piggy.' Then he called her 'Miss Housekeeping,' because she was Latina. Donald, she has a name … Her name is Alicia Machado … And she has become a U.S. citizen, and you can bet she's going to vote this November."

All is fair in politics, and if Hillary Clinton wanted to run a "war on women" campaign attack against Donald Trump, it would just mean she was following in the footsteps of previous Democratic candidates. Almost immediately, media outlets ran detailed, if thinly sourced and one-sided, front-page and top-of-the-newscast stories, some including previously taken photo shoots of Machado with an American flag. That meant these stories and photos were ready to go and waiting for Clinton to sound the alarm by mentioning her name. There was no daylight between actual Hillary Clinton campaign talking points and the stories that ran on front pages across the land.

Note how differently media outlets covered the story when it first broke in 1997. CNN began its report on Machado by saying, "When Alicia Machado of Venezuela was named Miss Universe nine months ago, no one could accuse her of being the size of the universe. But as her universe expanded, so did she, putting on nearly 60 pounds." CNN added, "Since winning the crown, the former Miss Venezuela went from 118 pounds to – well – a number that kept growing like the size of the fish that got away."

Trump told reporters, "Some people when they have pressure eat too much. Like me. Like Alicia." Critics wanted the pageant to drop her and take away her crown, but the pageant officials, including Trump, just encouraged her to get her weight down. CNN's report ended with Trump telling a "rowdy pool of reporters" that "a lot of you folks have weight problems. I hate to tell you."

But when Clinton brought up Machado's attack in the first debate, the *New York Times* put two of its top reporters on the case, and they wrote an article entitled, "Shamed and Angry: Alicia Machado, a Miss Universe Mocked by Donald Trump." NBC's *TODAY* bought the Clinton spin hook, line, and sinker, conducting an interview with Machado titled "Donald Trump Hasn't Changed since Fat-Shaming Me in 1996, Alicia Machado Says."

Within seventy-two hours of the debate, the LexisNexis database showed that major media outlets had run hundreds of stories using Clinton's framing of the story. It wasn't just that they ran the story – the Clinton campaign even set up conference calls with reporters – but that they covered it without skepticism.

A less compliant media might have noted that the Mexican attorney general's office said Machado was romantically involved and had a daughter with notorious drug lord José Gerardo Álvarez-Vázquez, also known as "El Indio." A less compliant media might have noted that a Venezuelan judge claimed Machado threatened to ruin his career and

The "fact-checking trend" meant that journalists wouldn't just get to determine which stories saw the light of day and which were killed; they would pick the angle and framing for the stories.

kill him in response to his indictment of her then boyfriend for murder. A less compliant media might have noted that Machado was accused – albeit never prosecuted – of driving the getaway car in that murder.

Clinton wanted to push the idea that Machado had become a US citizen recently and would be voting for her. This was a natural contrast to the Trump campaign, which expressed skepticism about current US immigration policy and whether it served American interests. Such obvious problems with Machado's story and the fact that Machado was walking proof of Trump's contention that America's immigration policy is broken were barely noted by the media.

LIES, DAMNED LIES, AND FACT-CHECKING

Beginning in the second term of the Bush administration, various media enterprises got the idea to do something called "fact-checking." Not just the type of fact-checking they should have been doing in Journalism 101, mind you. No, the reelection of Bush had disappointed many journalists, and there was a sense from them that the Bush administration was getting away with not telling the truth.

The "fact-checking trend" meant that journalists would gain more power. They wouldn't just get to determine which stories saw the light of day and which were killed or downplayed; they would pick the angle and framing for the stories and determine who was quoted and how. And through fact-checking, they would tell people what to think about claims made in these stories.

It shouldn't surprise anyone that the fact-checking enterprises issued their findings in a biased fashion, with the benefit of the doubt and contextual loopholes provided for Democratic politicians in a way that was closed off for Republicans. One typical example is that the Pulitzer-winning PolitiFact rated Barack Obama's (false) claim in support of his health care legislation, "If you like your health care plan, you can keep your health care plan," as some variation of true six times before Obama's reelection in 2012. After he was reelected, when they had to actually implement Obamacare, millions of Americans immediately lost their health insurance plans. A claim PolitiFact had called true half a dozen times became PolitiFact's 2013 "lie of the year."

Instead of killing off the fact-checking trend, the media incorporated it into its coverage of the 2016 general election campaign. For example, Donald Trump repeatedly said throughout his primary campaign that President Obama and Hillary Clinton were founders, cofounders, or MVPs of ISIS. He said it three times in January of 2016 alone. He said that Clinton and Obama "created" ISIS, that Clinton "invented" ISIS and was responsible for ISIS, and that Clinton should "take an award" as the "founder" of ISIS.

These claims went mostly unnoticed by the media while Donald Trump was defeating Republican opponents, even if they were made in nationally televised speeches and interviews. But when he made a similar claim again in August after the candidates had been nominated, all hell broke loose.

To be fair, Trump's speaking style couldn't be more removed from the anodyne and cautious political rhetoric journalists have grown accustomed to and demanded from Republicans in particular. This was a challenge for political journalists. Trump's sentences ran on into paragraphs. He avoided specificity or contradicted himself when he was specific.

His sentences trailed into other sentences. It was frustrating.

But it's not as if his point was that difficult to understand. He opposed the Obama administration's handling of the Middle East region and how it led to the rise of ISIS. That's a downright normal political attack. But the media for some reason decided Trump was arguing that Obama and Clinton had literally filed articles of incorporation for the group. And they treated this literal claim as a fact that needed to be debunked.

This led to some funny contradictory fact-checks, such as when Bloomberg fact-checked this claim as false on account of Abu Musab al-Zarqawi founding the group while CNN fact-checked the claim as false on account of Abu Bakr al-Baghdadi founding the group.

Politifact gave Trump a "Pants on Fire" rating, even after admitting that President Barack Obama's leadership in Iraq and Hillary Clinton's push to change regimes in Libya led to the explosion of ISIS. The group's ruling was based on its belief that Trump was being hyperliteral.

Radio host Hugh Hewitt practically begged Donald Trump to phrase his ISIS arguments differently. "I'd just use different language to communicate it," Hewitt told him. Trump responded, "But they wouldn't talk about your language, and they do talk about my language, right?" Again, Trump was exploiting the media's double standards for how politicians are allowed to talk.

There was no good reason to adopt a hyperliteral posture when checking Trump. Fact-checking organizations gave Hillary Clinton a wide amount of latitude on statements that were obviously not true.

People accuse their political opponents of being responsible for bad things all the time. Clinton accused Trump of being ISIS's top recruiter. Bush's CIA and NSA chief said Trump was a "recruiting sergeant" for ISIS. Former New York City mayor Rudy Giuliani said Hillary Clinton could be considered a "founding member of ISIS." Senators Elizabeth Warren of Massachusetts and Chris Murphy of Connecticut declared that Senate Republicans were arming ISIS. Carly Fiorina and Rick Santorum blamed ISIS on Obama and Clinton. Senator John McCain said Obama was directly responsible for the Orlando ISIS attack due to his failure to deal with the group. President Obama said that Republicans trying to prioritize Christian victims of ISIS were ISIS's most potent recruiting tool. Heck, President Obama and *Vanity Fair* even blamed George W. Bush for ISIS.

There was no good reason to adopt a hyperliteral posture when checking Trump, and it added to the belief that the media was behaving unfairly to Trump.

Meanwhile, fact-checking organizations gave Hillary Clinton a very wide amount of latitude on statements that quite obviously were not literally true. On her claim that she "never received nor sent any material that was marked classified," PolitiFact rated the statement "half true" over a month after it was reported that Clinton had herself sent a classified e-mail on her insecure e-mail server. PolitiFact later stealth-edited the fact-check to claim the statement was false after FBI director Jim Comey's press conference acknowledging as much, but how PolitiFact ever defended such a brazen lie says a lot about the organization's partisan double standards.

It's Only Crazy When Trump Says It

Perhaps nothing better illustrates the media's double standards during the 2016 campaign as well as the coverage of Hillary Clinton's health. Throughout August and early September, the Trump campaign and its supporters were focused on the belief that Hillary Clinton didn't have the mental or physical stamina to handle the presidency. They hyped a serious coughing attack at a rally and questioned why the media wouldn't cover it.

The media responded not by covering her health but rather by arguing that it was sexist to question her health. CNN ran a story headlined, "Clinton's Health Is Fine, but What about Trump?" It didn't explain how anyone was to know her health was fine. Sanjay Gupta, a former Clinton advisor who became a CNN medical reporter, agreed that her health was fine. A panel convened to discuss the issue wondered if Trump's health wasn't the problem.

Neither Trump nor Clinton was forthcoming about personal health, but there were signs that Clinton might have legitimate issues to explore. Clinton's e-mails revealed that she told the FBI she couldn't recall something more than three dozen times. It was unclear if this was related to the concussion and blood clot she suffered at the end of 2012 limiting her productivity.

The *Washington Post*'s Chris Cillizza, who had written extensively about his belief that John McCain had serious health problems in 2008, wrote a piece defending Clinton against questions about her health. It was headlined, "Can We Just Stop Talking about Hillary Clinton's Health Now?" and was published on September 6. (John McCain was reelected to the Senate in 2016 by the way.)

Less than a week after Cillizza begged people to stop talking about Hillary Clinton's health, she had to leave a 9/11 commemoration due to health problems. She struggled to make her way to a van and passed out before she could climb in. Aides threw her in the vehicle and drove off. The campaign's story changed throughout the day. At first, she had merely tripped. Then she had become overcome by heat, despite it being a relatively cool day. Later she did a photo opportunity that featured her hugging a little girl. Later came the news she had been diagnosed with pneumonia. At each point of the story changing, the media largely reacted uncritically to what people had seen.

Another double standard was in how the media covered Donald Trump's answer in the final debate to a question about whether he'd certify the results of the election if he didn't win. He said he'd wait and see how things went. For a solid seventy-two hours, the media reaction was nothing but outrage. Yet when Hillary Clinton failed to win the election and joined legal recount efforts, and her supporters reacted with everything from riots to a months-long campaign of delegitimization, the media wasn't concerned at all.

THE END OF OUR
COLLECTIVE AMNESIA

In November of 2014, *Rolling Stone* published a cover story built around the claim that a woman had been raped by fraternity members at the University of Virginia. Sabrina Erdely's story was the latest piece of journalism to push the idea of a rape epidemic on campuses. While the story was initially met with widespread acclaim and resulted in the University of Virginia suspending the fraternity in question, it was later revealed to have been based on a false account that had been irresponsibly hyped by the reporter.

The magazine retracted the piece a few months later after the Columbia Graduate School of Journalism lambasted *Rolling Stone* for failing to uphold basic journalistic standards. The magazine's publisher and the reporter are fighting defamation lawsuits.

What the *Rolling Stone* debacle showed was the fraudulence of the media's claims about adherence to checking details and upholding standards. This was also on display in the aftermath of Trump's election when reporters reacted by running stories that turned out to be false or grossly mischaracterized.

Following Trump's surprising win, the *Washington Post* had a great idea. They asked his supporters why they voted for him. Among the many interesting answers were several that specifically mentioned the media: Nicole Citro said, "As Trump cleared each hurdle during the campaign, and I saw how the media, the establishment and celebrities tried to derail him, my hope began to grow that I would be able to witness their collective heads explode when he was successful." Diane Maus's answer was, "The media did the United States a huge disservice in covering this campaign." As Lori Myers explained, "I voted for Donald Trump because the media was so incredibly biased. They were unhinged in their obvious role as the Clinton campaign propaganda machine. The collusion was just too much." And Samantha Styler said, "I am a gay millennial woman and I voted for Donald Trump because I oppose the political correctness movement, which has become a fascist ideology of silence and ignorance. After months of going back and forth, I decided to listen to him directly and not through minced and filtered quotes from the mainstream media."

Perhaps these examples show that we've

entered the final stages of the longstanding social compact between voters and the media. It's not just that much of the country no longer trusts the media – the fact that Donald J. Trump is president is proof enough of that. It's also that, in a rather ironic twist of fate, the actual facts make it impossible to trust the media. After the University of Virginia story, can anyone still view *Rolling Stone* as reliable? And there's the gnawing suspicion that *Rolling Stone* is just the one that happened to get caught. Who knows what other publications have gotten away with that we don't know about?

Put another way, what we might be seeing is the end of the Murray Gell-Mann Amnesia effect. That was Michael Crichton's explanation, in his "Why Speculate?" speech, for why media carried a totally undeserved credibility. As Crichton explained:

Briefly stated, the Gell-Mann Amnesia effect is as follows. You open the newspaper to an article on some subject you know well. In Murray's case,

*physics. In mine, show business. You read the
article and see the journalist has absolutely no
understanding of either the facts or the issues.
Often, the article is so wrong it actually presents
the story backward – reversing cause and effect.
I call these the "wet streets cause rain" stories.
Paper's full of them. In any case, you read with
exasperation or amusement the multiple errors
in a story, and then turn the page to national or
international affairs, and read as if the rest of
the newspaper was somehow more accurate
about Palestine than the baloney you just read.
You turn the page, and forget what you know.*

Crichton went on to note that people tend to
exercise discretion in discounting serial liars
or exaggerators in other areas of life. And in
courts of law, there is a doctrine of *Falsus in
uno, falsus in omnibus.* "But when it comes to
the media," he said, "we believe against evidence that it is probably worth our time to
read other parts of the paper. When, in fact,
it almost certainly isn't."

But what if the errors are now so routine,

the narrative persuasion so blatant, the defensive defiance and elitism of journalists so extreme, and the partisan bias so pronounced that people are no longer slipping into amnesia? What if they're just done—sick and tired of the entire media industry and distrustful of many of the stories they encounter on TV and in newspapers? What does it mean going forward?

Members of the media once enjoyed an elevated position – celebrity status, even – on the theory that they would behave responsibly with the power they had to police public conversations. They were to aim for objectivity, civility, and the provision of important and helpful information rather than just advance partisan narratives at the expense of facts.

By 2016, the reality was that while the Democrats supported the media more than the Republicans did, the credibility afforded the media by both groups was off a cliff.

Two weeks before the 2016 election, a Suffolk University/*USA Today* poll asked one thousand Americans what they thought was the primary threat to election integrity. The poll was conducted months after President Obama had started talking about Russian meddling in the election and weeks after the Office of the Director of National Intelligence officially blamed Russia for ties to the hacking of the Democratic National Committee's e-mail and the successful spearfishing operation of John Podesta.

Still, 45.5 percent of those polled chose "the media" as the primary threat to election integrity. Only 10 percent chose "foreign interests such as Russian hackers."

That same poll showed that voters believed members of the media were aiding Hillary Clinton as the Democratic candidate for president. In fact, they were ten times more likely to say the media, including major newspapers and television stations, wanted Hillary Clinton to win.

Even earlier in 2016, trust in the media had hit historic lows.

Gallup reported in September 2016 that Americans' trust and confidence in the mass media "to report the news fully, accurately and fairly" dropped to its lowest level in polling history, with only 32 percent saying they have a great deal or fair amount of trust in the media. That was down eight points since the previous year. Among Republicans, the situation was much worse. Only 14 percent of them had confidence in the media.

Polls since the media began its claims of having a Trump-inspired renaissance have shown a slight uptick in Democratic support, but that only supports the idea that the media is composed of partisan actors whose interests align with Democrats and are hostile to Republicans.

As partisan actors, they lose their power to mediate public debates and discussions. Their claim to have anonymous sources who should be trusted is lost. The public now sees the major mass media as tabloids and scandal sheets that act as propaganda organs for a political party. The media's credibility is gone. And they did it to themselves.

While some might see the fact that Trump

portends the end of the hated liberal-media consensus as cause for celebration, this is also cause for concern. The media has long

---

The public now sees the major mass media as tabloids and scandal sheets that act as propaganda organs for a political party.

---

been an important check on the exercise of power of elected leaders. If the media does believe that it has an important role to play in holding elected leaders accountable, it only has one choice: Renounce partisanship, report the facts, stop pushing narratives, diversify newsrooms culturally and intellectually, and slowly but surely recover its credibility one honest report at a time. If the nascent coverage of the Trump administration is anything to go by, the media is uninterested in doing self-examination and the hard work this requires. Even Trump's fiercest critics are fed up with the media's impotence resulting from its bias and incompetence. "Much of the reporting on the Trump administration thus far seems to be so poorly sourced, riddled with caricature and negative wishful thinking as to be actively misleading, for all intents and purposes 'fake news,'" wrote Trump-critic James Kirchick in *Tablet*. "The beneficiary of the resulting confusion and hysteria is not *The New York Times* or its readers. It's Donald Trump." Kirchick is right, but after decades of systematic media bias, the biggest loser of all has been ordinary Americans. Until the media at least acts like it respects the concerns of all Americans, regardless of whether they share its narrow progressive views, it is doomed to irrelevance in Donald Trump's America.

© 2017 by Mollie Ziegler Hemingway

First American edition published in 2017 by Encounter Books, an activity of Encounter for Culture and Education, Inc., a nonprofit, tax exempt corporation.
Encounter Books website address: www.encounterbooks.com

Manufactured in the United States and printed on acid-free paper. The paper used in this publication meets the minimum requirements of ANSI/NISO z39.48–1992 (R 1997) (*Permanence of Paper*).

FIRST AMERICAN EDITION

LIBRARY OF CONGRESS
CATALOGING-IN-PUBLICATION DATA
IS AVAILABLE

Names: Hemingway, Mollie Ziegler, author.
Title: Trump vs. the media / by Mollie Ziegler Hemingway.
Other titles: Trump versus the media
Description: New York : Encounter Books, 2017. |
Series: Encounter broadsides ; 51 | Description based on print version record and CIP data provided by publisher; resource not viewed.
Identifiers: LCCN 2017010507 (print) | LCCN 2017011990 (ebook) | ISBN 9781594039775 (Ebook) | ISBN 9781594039768 (pbk. : alk. paper)
Subjects: LCSH: Trump, Donald, 1946—In mass media. | Presidents—United States—Press coverage. | Mass media—Political aspects—United States. | Press and politics—History—21st century.
Classification: LCC E901.1.T78 (ebook) | LCC E901.1.T78 H46 2017 (print) | DDC 973.933092--dc23
LC record available at https://lccn.loc.gov/2017010507

10 9 8 7 6 5 4 3 2 1